John Bunyan 1628-1688

After a drawing from the Life by R. White
preserved in the British Museum

LESSONS FROM NATURE:

POEMS FOR BOYS & GIRLS

BY JOHN BUNYAN

Back Home Industries
P.O. Box 22495
Milwaukie, Oregon 97269-2495

Bunyan's Poems first published posthumously
in London in 1701

This reprint, with added introduction and graphics, is based
on the 1724 edition of Bunyan's work
© Back Home Industries, 1998, 2000

All rights reserved. No part of this book may be reproduced or transmitted in any form or by any means without permission in writing from the Publisher.

Printed in the United States of America
Library of Congress Catalog Card Number 98-70028

ISBN 1-880045-19-2

LESSONS FROM NATURE:

POEMS FOR BOYS AND GIRLS

by JOHN BUNYAN

Edited by Gary and Wanda Sanseri, 1998

The original work was entitled

A BOOK FOR BOYS AND GIRLS:

TEMPORAL THINGS SPIRITUALIZED

by JOHN BUNYAN

R. Tookey, at his Print House in St. Christopher's Court, in Threadneedle Street, behind the Royal Exchange, London, England, 1701.

The 1998 reprint comes from a later printing

DIVINE EMBLEMS:

TEMPORAL THINGS SPIRITUALIZED

Fitted for the Use of Boys and Girls

by JOHN BUNYAN.

Printed by S. Negris, for John Marshall, at the Bible, in Gracechurch Street, London 1724

LESSONS FROM NATURE: POEMS FOR BOYS AND GIRLS

TABLE OF CONTENTS

Foreword by Editor of 1875 Edition..................8
Foreword by Editor of 1998 Edition..................12
Bunyan Inspires Contemporary Youth..................17
Bunyan's Preface..................20

1	The Barren Fig-Tree in God's Vineyard	27
2	The Vine	29
3	The Promising Fruitfulness of a Tree	31
4	The Rosebush	33
5	Meditations upon an Egg	35
6	The Cackling of a Hen	39
7	The Swallow	40
8	The Cuckoo	41
9	Fowls Flying in the Air	43
10	The Child's Offer to a Bird	47
11	The Lark and the Fowler	51
12	The Boy and Butterfly	53
13	The Sinner and the Spider	55
14	The Bee	65
15	The Ant	67
16	The Fish in the Water	69
17	The Flint in the Water	71
18	The Mole in the Ground	72
19	The Frog	73
20	The Day before the Sunrising	75

Lessons from Nature: Poems for Boys and Girls

21	The Peep of Day	76
22	The Rising of the Sun	77
23	A Lowering Morning	78
24	Clouds in a Fair Morning	79
25	Going Down of the Sun	80
26	A Snail	81
27	A Skillful Player on an Instrument	83
28	A Fire	85
29	A Candle	86
30	The Fly at the Candle	91
31	A Pound of Candles Falling to the Ground	93
32	The Spinning of a Top	95
33	A Penny Loaf	96
34	The Beggar	97
35	The Thief	99
36	The Horse and His Rider	101
37	A Sheet of White Paper	103
38	The Boy and Watchmaker	105
39	An Hour Glass	107
40	Over-much Niceness	108
41	Apparel	109
42	A Looking Glass	110
43	Man by Nature	111
44	The Disobedient Child	112
45	The Love of Christ	115
46	Moses and His Wife	118
47	The Spouse of Christ	119
48	The Sacraments	122
49	The Lord's Prayer in Rhyme	123

BUNYAN'S DIVINE EMBLEMS

FOREWORD BY EDITOR OF 1875 EDITION

Some degree of mystery hangs over these *Divine Emblems* for children, and many years' diligent research has not enabled me completely to solve it. That they were written by Bunyan, there cannot be the slightest doubt.

'Manner and matter, too, are all his own.'[1]

No book, under the title of *Divine Emblems* is mentioned in any catalogue or advertisements of Bunyan's works, published during his life; nor in those more complete lists printed by his personal friends, immediately after his death.

In all these lists, as well as in many advertisements, both before, and shortly after Mr. Bunyan's death, a little book for children is constantly introduced, which, judging from the title, must have been similar to, if not the same as, these Emblems; but the Editor has not been able to discover a copy of the first edition, although every inquiry has been made for it, both in the United Kingdom and America.

It was advertised in 1688, as *Country Rhymes for Children*, upon seventy-four things.[2] It is also advertised, in the same year, as *A Book for Boys and Girls*, or *Country Rhymes for Children*, price 6d.[3] In 1692, it is included in Charles Doe's catalogue table of all Mr. Bunyan's books, appended to *The Struggler for their preservation, No. 36; Meditations on seventy-four things*, published in 1685, and not reprinted during the author's life. In Charles Doe's second catalogue of all Mr. Bunyan's books, appended to the first edition of the *Heavenly Footman*, March 1698, it is No. 37. *A Book for Boys and Girls*, or *Country Rhymes for Children*, in verse, on seventy-four things. This catalogue describes every work, word for word, as it is in the several title pages.

In 1707 it had reached a third edition, and was 'ornamented with cuts;'[4] and the title is altered to *A Book for Boys and Girls, or Temporal Things Spiritualized.* In 1720, it was advertised, 'price, bound, 6d.'[5] In *Keach's Glorious Lover*, it is advertised by Marshall, in 12mo. price 1s. In 1724, it assumed the title and from that time was repeatedly advertised as *Divine Emblems*, or *Temporal Things Spiritualized*, fitted for the use of boys and girls.

By indefatigable exertions, my excellent friend and brother collector of old English Bibles, James Dix, Esq., Bristol, has just discovered and presented to me the second edition of this very rare little volume, in fine preservation, from which it appears, that in 1701, the title page was altered from *Country Rhymes and Meditations*, to *A Book for Boys and Girls*, or *Temporal Things Spiritualized.* It contains exactly the same subjects as the subsequent editions published under the more popular title *Divine Emblems.*

The only difficulty that remains is to discover seventy-four meditations in the forty-nine emblems. This may be readily done, if the subjects of meditation are drawn out. Thus, one emblem contains meditations on two things, *the Barren Fig Tree*, and *God's Vineyard*. Another has a meditation on *the Lark and the Fowler*, and another on the comparison between *the Fowler and Satan*. Upon this plan, the volume contains exactly seventy-four meditations.

Under the title of *Divine Emblems*, **it has passed through a multitude of editions, and many thousand copies have been circulated.** It was patronized in those early efforts of the Religious Tract Society, which have been so abundantly blessed in introducing wholesome food to the young, instead of the absurd romances which formerly poisoned the infant and youthful mind.

Among these numerous editions, two deserve special notice. The first of these was published in 1757, 'on a curious paper, and good letter, with new cuts.' It has a singular preface, singed J. D., addressed 'to the great Boys, in folio, and the little ones in coats.' The first eight pages give a dissertation on the origin of language, perhaps arising from a line in the dialogue between a sinner and spider, ' My name entailed is to my creation.' In this preface, he learnedly attempts to prove that language was the gift of God by revelation, and not a gradual acquirement of man as his wants multiplied.

The other remarkable edition was published about 1790.[6] It is, both the text and cuts, printed from copperplate engravings, very handsomely executed. This is an honor conferred upon very few authors;[7] nor was it ever conferred upon one more worthy the highest veneration of man than is the immortal allegorist.

The number of editions which have been printed of these little engaging poems, is a proof of the high estimation in which they have been held for nearly one hundred and seventy years; and the great rarity of the early copies shows the eager interest with which they have been read by children until utterly destroyed.

The cuts [illustrations] were at first exceedingly coarse and rude, but were much improved in the more modern copies.

Those to Mason's edition are handsome. The engraver dressed all his actors in the costume of the time of George the Third; the women with hooped petticoats and high head dresses; clergymen with five or six tier wigs; men with cocked hats and queues; and female servants with mob caps. That to the on the sacraments, is peculiarly droll; the artist, forgetting that the author was a Baptist, represents a baby brought to the font to be christened! and two persons kneeling before the body of our Lord!

GEO. OFFOR.
1875

---

1. Bunyan's poem in the Holy War.
2. On the leaf following the title to *One Thing is Needful, &c.*, by John Bunyan, 1688. A rare little 32mo, published by the author, in possession of the Editor.
3. *At the end of Grace Abounding,* the sixth edition, and also in *The Work of Jesus Christ as an Advocate,* by Bunyan, 1688.
4. Advertised in the eighth edition of *Solomon's Temple Spiritualized.*
5. In *Youth Directed and Instructed* a curious little book for children.
6. Square 24mo, by Bennet, Burney, and others, without date.
7. Sturt engraved the *Book of Common Prayer*; some French artists elegantly etched two of their devotional books; and Pyne engraved the texts of Horace and Virgil with beautiful vignettes.

FORWARD BY EDITOR OF 1998 EDITION

Most readers will know of John Bunyan as the author of the Christian classic, *The Pilgrim's Progress*. Bunyan was born in the year 1628 in a village called Elstow near Bedford, England. He followed in his father's trade as a tinker.

In 1644, during the English Civil Wars, Bunyan enlisted in the Parliamentary army to defend the Protestant cause against King Charles I and his royalist forces. After being discharged from the army in 1647, Bunyan resumed his trade in Elstow.

In 1649 he married a young woman probably named Mary. She brought to their marriage two important books, left to her at the death of her father: Arthur Dent's, *The Plain Man's Path-Way to Heaven* and Lewis Bayley's, *The Practice of Piety*. By reading these books, Bunyan became convinced of his sinfulness and condemnation to the flames of hell. Later Bunyan confessed, "these books did beget within me some desire to religion."

After numerous attempts to reform his life, Bunyan began to direct his attention to an intense study of the Bible. Great help came to him from Luther's *Commentary on Galatians* which Bunyan felt was written from "out of his own heart." Several years after joining an Independent church in Bedford, Bunyan came to know the assurance of the forgiveness of sins and his election by God as His own dear child.

Around 1652 Bunyan began to preach in public. In the 17th century unlicensed preachers, like Bunyan, were not well received. Their frequent rewards included humiliation and imprisonment. In 1658 Bunyan's first wife died leaving him four children. He then married Elizabeth, his second wife, in 1659.

Bunyan's reasonable freedom under Oliver Cromwell, the Protector, came to an end in 1660 at the restoration of the kingdom to Charles II. He was arrested in 1660 for his non-compliance to religious restrictions soon to become law under The Act of Uniformity, which among other things, rejected all preachers but those ordained by bishops of the established Church of England. His specific crime was preaching without a license to unlawful assemblies. He spent most of his next 12 years of life in a prison cell in Bedford.

While in prison, Bunyan kept busy making shoe laces to sell for the support of his family, preaching to his fellow inmates and taking up his pen and writing books which would immortalize the tinker of Bedford in the annals of history. His first prison book (1661) he entitled, *Profitable Meditations*. This was followed by *I Will Pray with the Spirit* (1662), *Christian Behavior* (1663), *The Holy City* (1665) and his all important autobiography, *Grace Abounding* (1666).

Following the Declaration of Indulgence in 1672, Bunyan was released from prison and became a licensed preacher and pastor of the Bedford congregation. This declaration, however, was later revoked and Bunyan again found himself in jail. During this second imprisonment he wrote part one of his famous book, *The Pilgrim's Progress*.

Bunyan died August 31, 1688 as a result of a fever

contracted in heavy rain during a journey from Reading to London. While conducting Bunyan's funeral, George Cokayan preached these memorable words:

> It is remarkably strange that this man who came into the world under such poor circumstances and lived a portion of his life under the most handicapped conditions did such a great work. Nearly twelve years he spent in Bedford Jail as a religious prisoner, suffering for the freedom he craved.
>
> He lived almost sixty years and leaves behind him exactly sixty books-a book for every year of his life. His latest book is now awaiting publication in this city and will doubtless be read by thousands as his last message to his fellowmen....
>
> Bunyan was not only loved by the common people but was revered and respected by even the most wealthy and educated.... The candle which John Bunyan has lighted in England shall never be put out. Above all his other works, *Pilgrim's Progress* already has gone far enough over many lands to see that it may become one of England's greatest contributions to the literature of this century....

The book now in the reader's hands first appeared under the title, *A Book for Boys and Girls* or, *Country Rhymes for Children.* The third edition of the book, in 1707, bore the title, *A Book for Boys and Girls,* or *Temporal Things Spiritualized.* In 1724 the book was advertised as *Divine Emblems,* or *Temporal Things Spiritualized.*

Apparently, after these early editions, no copy of the

book was known to exist until one was sold to America in 1888. This copy was then resold to the British Museum Library, where it is now deposited. According to Frank Mott Harrison, "another copy unexpectedly discovered in 1926, was offered by auction in London and purchased for America at the astonishing sum of two thousand guineas!" This current publication uses the title, *Lessons from Nature: Poems for Boys and Girls.*

Bunyan's 19th century biographer, John Brown, says, regarding *A Book for Boys and Girls*, "The book which is in rhyme, rises here and there to poetry, and everywhere is marked by good sense and wise intent, making up altogether a collection of such similes as were ever coming to the writer's mind like ripples over a stream."

This reprint is published with the intention of helping young boys and girls formulate Christian ideals as they live in this present world.

Minimal changes have been made in the text to help clarify archaic words or adjust the rhyme to match modern pronunciation. For example Bunyan had as rhymes *do* and *go*. In order to provide an attractive, easily readable edition, we divided long continuous text into smaller units. We have also added questions and Scripture references to help facilitate discussion of the poems. We did not consider the graphics added to the 1724 edition effective in illustrating the poems. Instead we have used copyright free clip art of children and animals to make this work come alive with action and interest. We trust you will enjoy this little volume and that the Lord will be glorified.

--Gary Sanseri, 1998

Lessons from Nature: Poems for Boys and Girls

Only an old drawing remains of the cottage
where John Bunyan was born.
The building itself disappeared
over one hundred and seventy years ago.

In Appreciation

BUNYAN POEMS INSPIRE CONTEMPORARY YOUNG WRITER

Mundy Alcala retyped the 1724 edition of Bunyan's poems for us, and we are grateful for her fast, accurate work. Meanwhile, her teenage daughter, Lisa enjoyed reading the manuscript and secretly composed her own allegorical poem using the pattern role modeled by John Bunyan.

Mundy handed me a copy of Lisa's poem without saying anything. On first glance I thought she had accidentally forgotten one of the poems by Bunyan and said something to that effect. "Bunyan didn't write that one," replied a beaming mother. "Lisa did." Only later did I notice that Lisa's poem uses free verse while Bunyan employs various rhyme patterns. Poetic license provides for such flexibility. Her work is actually more contemporary this way.

We're delighted with Lisa's contribution and challenge other youth to try their own hand in composing comparisons between temporal object lessons and spiritual truths. Thank you Mundy and Lisa for your encouragement with this project! We also appretticate Violet Tse who edited the manuscript for us.

WINTER

The clouds are gray.
The wind is cold.
The rain is wet,
And the sun does not show.

Still we wait
Through the dreary winter long,
Holding on to the knowledge that
The bright face of glory will shine again!

Comparison

The believer's life on this world can be
Compared with the weary winter.
The gray clouds of sin come around us.
Winds of sorrow knock us down.

The rains of difficulty drench us.
But we have the blessed promise that,
Our Lord and Savior will come again
To take us home to be with Him!

by Lisa Alcala, March 1997

BUNYAN'S PREFACE

Written for All Ages

The title page will show, if there thou look,
Who are the proper subjects of this book.
They're boys and girls of all sorts and degrees,
From those of age to children on the knees.

Thus comprehensive am I in my notions,
They tempt me to it by their childish motions.
We now have boys with beards, and girls that be
Big[1] as old women, wanting gravity.

Then do not blame me, 'cause I thus describe them.
Flatter I may not, lest thereby I bribe men
To have a better judgment of themselves,
Than wise men have of babies on their shelves.[2]

Their antic tricks, fantastic modes, and way,
Show they, like very boys and girls, do play
With all the frantic fopperies[3] of this age,
And that in open view, as on a stage;
Our bearded men do act like beardless boys;
Our women please themselves with childish toys.

Appealing to the Young at Heart

Our ministers, long time, by word and pen,
Dealt with them, counting them not boys, but men.
Thunderbolts they shot at them and their toys,
But hit them not, 'cause they were girls and boys.

The better charged, the wider still they shot,
Or else so high, these dwarfs they touched not.
Instead of men, they found them girls and boys,
Addict to nothing as to childish toys.

Wherefore, good reader, that I save them may,
I now with them the very dotterel[4] play;
And since at gravity they make a tush,[5]
My very beard I cast behind a bush;
And like a fool stand fingering of their toys,
And all show them they are girls and boys.

Nor do I blush, although I think some may
Call me a baby, 'cause I with them play.
I want to show them how each fingle-fangle
On which they doting are, their souls entangle,
As with a web, a trap, a gin, or snare;
And will destroy them, have they not a care.

Lessons Not Confined to Childish Toys

Paul seemed to play the fool, that he might gain
Those that were fools indeed, if not in grain;[6]
And did it by their things, that they might know
Their emptiness, and might be brought in tow.
What would them save from sin and vanity,
A noble act, and full of honesty.

Yet he nor I would like them be in vice,
While by their playthings I would them entice,

To mount their thoughts from what are childish toys,
To heaven, for that's prepared for girls and boys.

Nor do I so confine myself to these,
As to shun graver thing; I seek to please
Those more composed with better things than toys;
Though thus I would be catching girls and boys.

Wherefore, if men have now a mind to look,
Perhaps their graver fancies may be took
With what is here, though but in homely rhymes:
But he who pleases all must rise betimes.

Some, I am sure, will be finding of fault,
Concluding, here I trip, and there I halt:

What though my test seems mean, my morals be
Grave, as if fetched from a sublimer tree.
And if some can better handle[7] a fly,
Than some a text, why should we then deny
Their making proof, or good experiment,
Of smallest things, great mischiefs to prevent?

Scripture Uses Object Lessons for Teaching

Wise Solomon did fools to small ants send,
To learn true wisdom, and their lives to mend.
Yea, God by swallows, cuckoos, and the ass,[8]
Shows they are fools who let that season pass,
Which he put in their hand, that to obtain
Which is both present and eternal gain.

I think the wiser sort my rhymes may slight,
But what care I, the foolish will delight
To read them, and the foolish God has chose,
And does by foolish things their minds compose,
And settle upon that which is divine;
Great things, by little ones, are made to shine.

I could, were I so pleased, use higher strains;
And for applause on tenters[9] stretch my brains.
But what needs that? the arrow, out of sight,
Does not the sleeper, nor the watchman fright;
To shoot too high does but make children gaze,
'Tis that which hits the man does him amaze.

And for the inconsiderableness
Of things, by which I do my mind express,
May I by them bring some good thing to pass,
As Samson, with the jawbone of an ass;[10]
Or as brave Shamgar, with his ox's goad[11]
(Both being things not manly, nor for war in mode),
I have my end, though I myself expose
To scorn; God will have glory in the close. J.B.

---

    1. altered to 'huge' in *The Emblems*, 1724.

    2. *of babies on their shelves*--A familiar phrase, denoting persons who have been always frivolous and childish, or those who have passed into second childhood. 'On the shelf' is a common saying of ladies when they are too old to get married.--(Ed. 1724.)

    3. *fopperies* - showing vanity with fine clothes and affected manners (Ed., 1998)

    4. *dotterel*--The name of a bird that mimics gestures.--(Ed.. 1998)

    5. *tush* - exclamation expressing impatience, contempt, etc. (Ed., 1998)

    6. *in grain*--indelible, as when raw material is dyed before it is wove, every grain receives the dye.--(Ed., 1724)

    7. For this use of the word 'handle,' see Jer. 2:8. 'They that handle the law."--(Ed., 1724)

    8. See Ps. 84: 3; Lev.11:16; Num.20.

    9. *tenters*--A machine used in the manufacture of cloth, on which it is stretched.--(Ed., 1724)

    10. Judges 15:15

    11. Judges 3:31

*Wise Solomon did fools to small ants send,
To learn true wisdom, and their lives to mend.*

*Yea, God by swallows, cuckoos, and the ass,
Shows they are fools who let that season pass,*

*Which he put in their hand, that to obtain
Which is both present and eternal gain.*

--John Bunyan

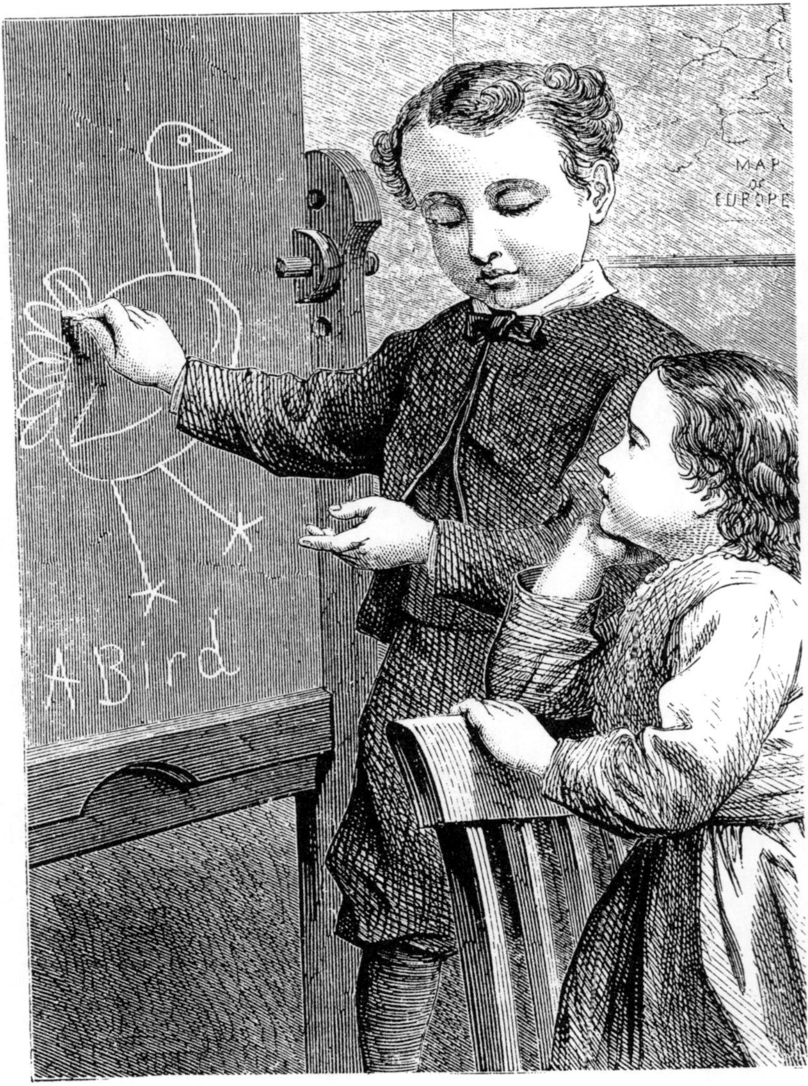
MAP
OF
EUROPE
A Bird

THE POEMS

"But, now ask the beasts,
    and they will teach you;
And the birds of the air,
    and they will tell you;
Or speak to the earth,
    and it will teach you;
And the fish of the sea
    will explain to you."
        --Job 12:7-8

I.

THE BARREN FIG-TREE
IN GOD'S VINEYARD

What, barren here! in this so good a soil?
The sight of this does make God's heart recoil
From giving thee his blessing; barren tree,
Bear fruit, or else your end will cursed be!

Art you not planted by the water-side?
Know not your Lord by fruit is glorified?
The sentence is, Cut down the barren tree:
Bear fruit, or else your end will cursed be!

Lessons from Nature: Poems for Boys and Girls

You have been digged about and dunged too,[1]
Will neither patience nor yet dressing do?
The executioner is come, O tree,
Bear fruit, or else your end will cursed be!

He that about your roots takes pains to dig,
Would, if on you were found but one good fig,
Preserve you from the axe: but, barren tree,
Bear fruit, or else your end will cursed be!

The utmost end of patience is at hand,
'Tis much if you much longer here do stand.
O hardened ground, you are a barren tree.
Bear fruit, or else your end will cursed be!

Thy standing nor thy name will help at all;
When fruitful trees are spared, thou must fall.
The axe is laid unto they roots, O tree!
Bear fruit, or else your end will cursed be!

---

1. *digged about and dunged too*--The soil broken up with fertilizer added.

Questions on Poem I

Q. 1. What happens to a tree that bears no fruit?

Q. 2. What kind of spiritual fruit can Christians bear?

II

THE VINE

A creeping vine is weaker than a tree,
Nay most, than it, more tall, more comely be.
A workman values a beam not a pin,
To make that which may be delighted in.

Its excellency in its fruit does lie:
A fruitless vine, it is not worth a fly.

Comparison

What are professors more than other men?
Nothing at all. Nay there's not one in ten,
Either for wealth, or wit, that may compare,
In many things, with some that carnal are.

Good are they, if they mortify their sin,
But without that, they have no worth within.

Questions on Poem II

Q.1. How is a vine different from a tree?

Q. 2. To the author what type of vine is worthless?

Q. 3. To whom does he compare to a fruitless vine?

III

THE PROMISING FRUITFULNESS OF A TREE

A comely sight indeed it is to see
A world of blossoms on an apple-tree:
Yet far more comely would this tree appear,
If all its dainty blooms brought apples here.

But how much more might one upon it see,
If all would hang there till they ripe should be.
But most of all its beauty would abound,
If no worm-eaten ones should there be found.

But we, alas! do commonly behold
Blooms fall quickly, if mornings be but cold.
They too, which grow to become apples there,
By blasting winds and vermin take despair,

Remaining fruit, while almost ripe, we see
By blust'ring winds are shaken from the tree,
So that of many, only some there be,
That grow till they come to maturity.

Comparison

This tree a perfect emblem is of those
Which God doth plant, which in his garden grows,
Its blasted blooms are motions unto good,
Which chill affections do nip in the bud.

Those little apples which yet blasted are,
Show some good purposes, no good fruits bear.
Those spoiled by vermin are to let us see,
How good attempts by bad thoughts ruined be.

Those that the wind blows down, while they are green,
Show good works have by trials spoiled been.[1]

Those that abide, while ripe upon the tree,
Show, in a good man, some ripe fruit will be.

Behold then how abortive some fruits are,
Which at the first most promising appear.
The frost, the wind, the worm, with time does show,
From promising appearance few works flow.

---

1. Use British pronunciation to say been.

Questions on Poem III

Q. 1. Compare the effect of the frost, wind, worm, and time on the spiritual fruitfulness of man.

Q. 2. What does Bunyan mean by the statement, "From promising appearance few works flow"?

IV

THE ROSEBUSH

This homely bush does to mine eyes expose
A very fair, yea, comely ruddy rose.
This rose does also bow its head to me,
Saying, Come, pluck me, I thy rose will be;

Yet offer I to gather rose or bud,
Ten to one but the bush will have my blood.
This looks like a trap, a kind of decoy,
To offer, and yet snap, who would enjoy;

Yea, the more eager to it, the more in danger,
Be he the master of it, or a stranger.
Bush, why bear thee a rose if none must have it,
Why expose it, yet claw those that crave it?

Art become freakish? does the wanton play,
Or does your testy humour tend its way?

Comparison

This rose God's Son is, with his ruddy looks.
But what's the bush, whose pricks, like tenter-hooks
Do scratch and claw the finest lady's hands,
Or rend her clothes, if she too near it stands?

This bush an emblem is of Adam's race,
Of which Christ come, when He His Father's grace
Commended to us in His crimson blood,
While He in sinners' stead and nature stood.

Thus Adam's race did bear this dainty rose,
And does the same to Adam's race expose;
But those of Adam's race which at it catch,
Adam's race will them prick, and claw, and scratch.

Questions on Poem IV

Q. 1. The comparison is made between the rose and what person?

Q. 2. What do the thorns represent?

V

MEDITATIONS UPON AN EGG

From Egg to Chick

The egg's no chick by falling from the hen;
Nor man a Christian, till he's born again.

The egg's at first contained in the shell;
Men, before grace, in sins and darkness dwell.

The egg, when laid, by warmth is made a chicken,
And Christ, by grace, those dead in sin does quicken.

The egg, when first a chick, the shell's it's prison;
So's flesh to the soul, who yet with Christ is risen.

The shell does crack, the chick does chirp and peep,
The flesh decays, as men do pray and weep.

The shell does break, the chick's at liberty,
The flesh falls off, the soul mounts up on high.

But both do not enjoy the self-same plight;
The soul is safe, the chick now fears the kite.[1]

---

1 The kite referred to here is a swallow-tailed kite, a bird of prey about two feet long which would love to eat a baby chick for dinner.

Questions on Poem V

Q. 1. How is an unconverted man like an egg in the shell?
Q. 2. Warmth for the chicken is compared to what?
Q. 3. How is an egg shell related to man's sinful flesh?
Q. 4. How is a cracked shell related to man's repentance?
Q. 5. How does the hatched chick represent redemption?
Q. 6. How is the hope of the believer better than the future for the chick?

A Rotten Egg

Chicks from rotten eggs do not proceed,
Nor is a hypocrite a saint indeed.

The rotten egg, though underneath the hen,
If cracked, stinks, and is loathsome unto men.

Nor does her warmth make what is rotten sound;
What's rotten, rotten will at last be found.

The hypocrite, sin has him in possession,
He is a rotten egg under profession.

Questions on Poem V
Q. 1. What is a hypocrite?
Q. 2. List three ways a hypocrite is like a rotten egg.

Divers Eggs Produce Diverse Shapes

Some eggs bring slithering **snakes** and some men
Seem hatched and brooded in the viper's den.[1]

Some eggs bring **wild-fowls**; and some men there be
As wild as are the wildest fowls that flee.

Some eggs bring **spiders**, and some men appear
More venomed than the worst of spiders here.

Some eggs bring **alligators** and some men
Are big mouthed and violent with hard tough skin.

Thus divers eggs do produce divers shapes,
As like some men as monkeys are like apes.

But this is but an egg, were it a chick,
Here had been legs, and wings, and bones to pick.

---

1. "Preserve me from violent men, who plan evil things in their hearts; they continually gather together for war. They sharpen their tongues like a serpent; the poison of asps is under their tongues." --Psalm 140: 1-3

Questions on Poem V

Q. 1. What are some diverse things born from eggs?
Q. 2. Name some other animal life born out of eggs.
Q. 3. What is the relationship between the words ape and monkey?
Q. 4. How does Bunyand compare man to the negative traits of some of these animals produced from eggs?

Lessons from Nature: Poems for Boys and Girls

snake

wild-fowl

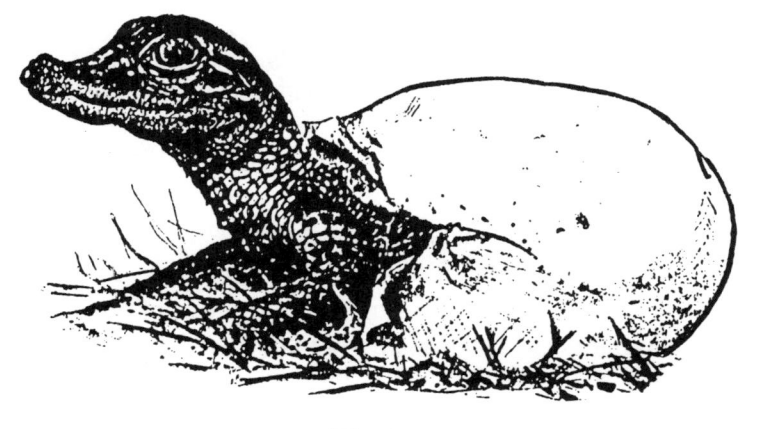

alligator

VI

THE CACKLING OF A HEN

The hen, so soon as she an egg does lay,
Spreads the fame of her doing what she may

About the yard she cackling now does go,
To tell to all what work she now did do.

Comparison

Just thus it is with some professing men,
If they do any good, just like our hen
They cackle of it wherever they go,
What their right hand does their left hand must know.

Questions on Poem VI
Q. 1. Why shouldn't believers imitate a cackling hen?
Q. 2. What does Bunyan mean by the last line?

VII

THE SWALLOW

This pretty bird, O! how she flies and sings,[1]
But could she do so if she had not wings?

Comparison

Her wings bespeak my faith, her songs my peace;
When I believe and sing my doubtings cease.

---

1. The swallow is remarkably swift in flight; 'their note is a slight twittering, which they seldom if ever exert but upon the wing.'--Goldsmith's Natural History.--(Ed.)

Questions on Poem VII

Q. 1. How is singing related to the flying of a swallow?
Q. 2. What does Bunyan compare to the swallow's wings? to her song?
Q. 3. In Jeremiah 8:7 the Lord uses the swallow in another way as an obejct lesson. What can we learn from the swallow? Can you enlarge the poem to include this idea?
Q. 4. Sparrows and swallows make their a nest in the eaves of buildings. Where did these birds locate their nests in Psalm 84? Can you also write a section in the poem adding an application based on this passage of Scripture?

VIII

OF THE CUCKOO

Thou booby, say you nothing but Cuckoo?
The robin and the wren can you outdo.
They to us play thorough their little throats,
Taking not one, but sundry pretty sounding notes.

But you poor fellows, some like you can do
Little but suck our eggs, and sing Cuckoo.
Your notes do not first welcome in our spring,
Nor do you its first tokens to us bring.

Birds less than you by far, like prophets, do
Tell us, 'tis coming, though not by Cuckoo.
Nor do you summer have away with thee,
Though you a yowling bawling Cuckoo be.

When you do cease among us to appear,
Then does our harvest bravely crown our year.
But you poor fellows, some like you can do
Little but suck our eggs, and sing Cuckoo.

The Cuckoos forward not our early spring,
Nor help with notes for harvest in to bring;
And while with us she only makes a noise,
Not pleasing unto you as girls and boys.

Comparison

The Formalist we may compare her to,
For he does suck our eggs, and sing Cuckoo.

The Cuckoo Bird

A cuckoo is a large song bird whose call sounds much like its name. The common European cuckoo lays its eggs in other birds' nests instead of hatching them itself. The cuckoo clock makes the sound like the European cuckoo.

Questions on Poem VIII

Q. 1. Why does Bunyan dislike the cuckoo bird?

Q. 2. Who is a formalist and why does Bunyan dislike him?

IX

FOWLS FLYING IN THE AIR

Methinks I see a sight most excellent,
All sorts of birds fly in the firmament:

Some great, some small, all of a divers kind,
Mine eye affecting, pleasant to my mind.

Look how they tumble in the wholesome air,
Above the world of worldlings, and their care.

And as they divers are in bulk and hue,
So are they in their way of flying too.

So many birds, so many various things
Tumbling in the element upon their wings.

The eagle can have a wing span of 8 feet!

The pheasant, including the tail, is about 3 feet long

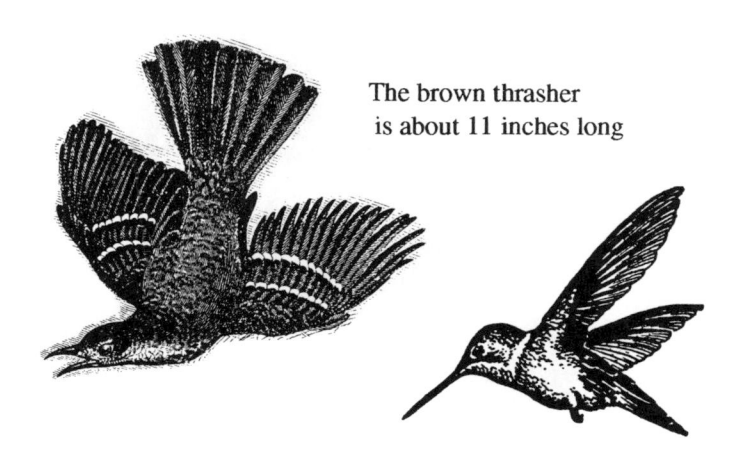

The parrot is about 15 inches long

The brown thrasher is about 11 inches long

The tiny hummingbird is less than 4 inches long! (See Ezekiel 17:3)

Comparison

These birds are emblems of those men that shall
Ere long possess the heavens, their all in all.

They are each of a diverse shape and kind,
To teach we of all nations there shall find.

They are some great, some little, as we see,
To show some great, some small, in glory be.

Their flying diversely, as we behold,
Do show saints' joys will there be manifold;

Some glide, some mount, some flutter, and some do,
In a mixed way of flying, glory too.

And all to show each saint, to his content,
Shall roll and tumble in the firmament.

a pelican   a flamingo

Lessons from Nature: Poems for Boys and Girls

Racket-tailed hummingbird

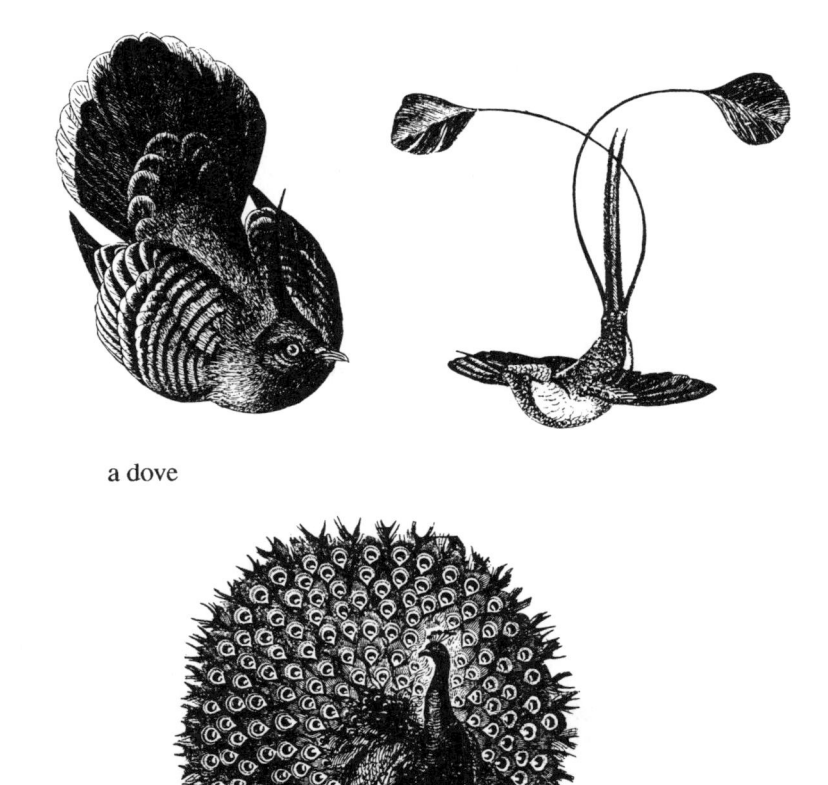

a dove

a peacock

Questions on Poem IX

Q. 1. How does the variety of birds compare to the variety of people who will populate heaven (Rev. 5:11 and 11:8)?

Q. 2. What are ways that birds differ according to Bunyan? Can you name other ways that birds are different?

X

THE CHILD'S OFFER TO A BIRD

My little bird, how can you sit
And sing amid so many thorns?
Let me hold upon you get,
My love with honor you adorns.

You are at present little worth,
Five farthings none will give for thee,
But pray thee, little bird, come forth,
You of more value art to me.

'Tis true it is sunshine today,
Tomorrow birds will have a storm;
My pretty one, come you away,
My bosom then shall keep you warm.

You subject are to cold at nights,
When darkness is your covering;
At days your danger's great by kites
How can you then sit there and sing?

A kite, a bird of prey

Your food is scarce and scanty too,
'Tis worms and trash which you do eat;
Your present state I pity do,
Come, I'll provide you better meat.

I'll feed you good with bread and milk,
And sugar plumbs, if them you crave.
I'll cover you with finest silk,
That from the cold I may you save.

My father's palace shall be thine,
Yea, in it you shalt sit and sing;
My little bird, if you'lt be mine,
The whole year round shall be your spring.

I'll teach you all the notes at court,
Unthought of music you shall play;
And all that thither do resort,
Shall praise you for it every day.

I'll keep you safe from cat and cur,
No manner of harm shall come to thee;
Yea, I will be thy succourer,
My bosom shall thy cabin be.

But lo, behold, the bird is gone;
These charmings would not make her yield;
The child's left at the bush alone,
The bird flies yonder o'er the field.

Comparison

This child of Christ an emblem is,
The bird to sinners I compare,
The thorns are like those sins of his
Which do surround him everywhere.

Her songs, her food, and sunshine day,
Are emblems of those foolish toys,
Which to destruction lead the way,

Questions on Poem X

Q. 1. How does Bunyan liken the child to Christ?
Q. 2. How is mankind in general likened to the bird?

Lessons from Nature: Poems for Boys and Girls

But lo, behold, the bird is gone!

    Editors Note: Notice the change in rhyme scheme in this poem from the previous ones. Here each line has eight beats and alternate lines rhyme. Earlier poems have ten beats per line and every two lines rhyme. Also notice the difference in indentations. Be watching for different poetic forms as you continue to study Bunyan's poems.

XI

THE LARK AND THE FOWLER

You simple bird, what makes you here to play?
Look, there's the fowler, pray you come away.
Do'st not behold the net? Look there, 'tis spread,
Venture a little further, you art dead.

Is there not room enough in all the field
For you to play, but you foolishly yield
To the deceitful glittering of a glass,
Placed betwixt nets, to bring your death to pass?

Bird, if you are so much for dazzling light,
Look, there's the sun above you; dart upright;
Your nature is to soar up to the sky,
Why will you come down to the nets and die?

Take no heed to the fowler's tempting call;
This whistle, he enchants birds withal.
Or if you see a live bird in his net,
Believe she's there, 'cause hence she cannot get.

Look how he tempts you with his decoy,
That he may rob you of your life, your joy.
Come, pray thee bird, I pray thee come away,
Why accept this net, when escape you may?

Had you not wings, or were your feather pulled,
Or were you blind, or fast asleep when lulled,
The case would somewhat alter, but for thee,
Your eyes are open, and you have wings to flee,

Remember that your song is in your rise,
Not in your fall; earth's not your paradise.
Keep up aloft, then, let your circuits be
Above, where birds from fowler's nets are free.

Comparison

This **fowler** is an emblem of the devil,
His nets and whistle, figures of all evil.
His glass an emblem is of sinful pleasure,
And his decoy of who counts sin a treasure.

This simple **lark's** a shadow of a saint,
Under allurings, ready now to faint.

This **admonisher** wants to teach you this,
That you avoid the snare and gain the bliss,
Learn how you may this fowler's net escape,
And not commit upon yourself this rape.

Questions on Poem XI

Q. 1. What is a fowler? See Psalm 91:3; 124:7-8.
Q. 2. What tricks do a fowler use to catch prey?
Q. 3. Who is compared to the fowler? the lark? the writer?

XII

THE BOY AND BUTTERFLY

Behold how eager this our little boy
Is for this Butterfly, as if all joy,
All profit, and hope, all lasting pleasure,
Were wrapped up in her, his richest treasure.

Found in her, would be bundled up together,
When all her all is lighter than a feather.
He halloos, runs, and cries out, Here, boys, here,
Nor does he brambles or the nettles fear.

He stumbles at the mole-hills, up he gets,
And runs again, as one bereft of wits;
And all this labour and this large outcry,
Is only for a silly butterfly.

Comparison

This little boy an emblem is of those
Whose hearts are wholly at the world's dispose.
The butterfly does represent to me,
The world's best things at best but fading be.

All are but painted nothings and false joys,
Like this poor butterfly to these our boys.
His running through nettles, thorns, and briars,
To gratify his boyish fond desires;

His tumbling over mole-hills to attain
His end, namely, his butterfly to gain;
Does plainly show what hazards some men run,
To get what will be lost as soon as won.

Men seem in choice, than children far more wise,
Because they run not after butterflies;
When yet, alas! for what are empty toys,
They follow children, like beardless boys.

Lessons from Nature: Poems for Boys and Girls

Questions on Poem XII

Q. 1. What does the author think about the boy's efforts to catch the butterfly?
Q. 2. What does Bunyan liken to the boy?
Q. 3. How are grown men different from the boy and the butterfly? like the boy and the butterfly?
Q. 4. What pursuit would Bunyan recommend?

Editor: He of riper years who seeks happiness in sensual gratification, is a child in understanding: he only changes his toys.

XIII

THE SINNER AND THE SPIDER

Sinner:

What black, what ugly crawling thing are you?

Spider:

I am a spider------

Sinner:

A spider, ay, also a filthy creature.

Spider:

Nor filthy as yourself in name or feature.
My name entailed is to my creation,
My features from the God of your salvation.

Sinner:

I am a man, and in God's image made,
I have a soul shall neither die nor fade,
God has endowed me with human reason.

Speak not against me less you speak treason.
For if I am the image of my Maker,
Of slanders laid on me He is partaker.

Spider:

I know you are a creature far above me,
Therefore I shun, I fear, and also love thee.
But though your God has made you such a creature,
Traitor to Him is your saddest feature.

A silk spider from Malaysia of the genus Naphila (male above, female below.)

Your sin has fetched you down at a great cost;
Nature you have defiled, God's image lost.
Yea, you yourself a very beast have made,
And are become like grass, which soon does fade.

Your soul, your reason, yea, your spotless state,
Sin has subjected to the most dreadful fate.
But I retain my primitive condition,
I've all but what I lost by thy ambition.

Sinner:

You venomed thing, I know not what to call thee,
The dregs of nature surely did befall thee,
You were made of the dross and scum of all,
Man hates you; does, in scorn, you spider call.

Spider:

My venom's good for something, 'cause God made it,
Of human virtues, therefore, though I fear thee,
I will not, though I might, despise and jeer thee.

You say I am the very dregs of nature,
Your sin's from Satan, not any creature.
You say man hates me 'cause I am a spider,
Poor man, you at your God are a derider;

My venom tends to my preservation,
Your pleasing follies work out your damnation.
Poor man, I keep the rules of my creation,
Your sin has cast you headlong from your station.

I hurt no one willingly, unlike you,
Self-murder you commit as fools will do.
Evil, not in good, do you now revel,
Defy God and adhere to the devil.

Lessons from Nature: Poems for Boys and Girls

A type of trapdoor spider

Sinner:

Ill-shaped creature, there's no great big tie
'Twixt man and spiders, 'tis in vain to lie;
I hate thee, stand off, if you do come nigh me,
I'll crush you with my foot; I do defy thee.

Spider:

They are ill-shaped, who warped are by sin,
A strong dislike in you has long time been
To God; no marvel then if me, his creature,
You do defy, pretending name and feature.

But why stand off? My presence shall not throng thee,
'Tis not my venom, but your sin does wrong thee.
Come, I will teach you wisdom, do but hear me.
I was made for your profit, do not fear me.

But if your God you will not hearken to,
What can the swallow, ant, or spider do?
Yet I will speak, I can but be rejected,
Sometimes great things by small means are effected.

Hark, then, though man is noble by creation,
He's lapsed now to such degeneration,
Is so besotted and so careless grown,
As not to grieve though he has overthrown
Himself, and brought to bondage everything
Created, from the spider to the king.

This we poor sensitives do feel and see;
For subject to the curse you made us be.
Tread not upon me, neither from me go;
'Tis man which has brought all the world to woe.

The law of my creation bids me teach thee;
I will not for your pride to God impeach thee.

I spin, I weave, and all to let you see,
Your best performances but cobwebs be.

Your glory now is brought to such an ebb,
It does not much excel the spider's web;
My webs becoming snares and traps for flies,
Do set the wiles of hell before your eyes;

Their tangling nature is to let you see,
Your sins too of a tangling nature be.
My den, or hole, for that 'tis bottomless,
Does of damnation show the lastingness.

My lying quiet until the fly is catch'd,
Shows secretly hell has your ruin hatch'd.
In that I on her seize, when she is taken,
I show who gather whom God has forsaken.

The fly lies buzzing in my web to tell
You how the sinners roar and how in hell.
These mysteries exposed before your eyes,
How can you hate me, or still scandalize?

Sinner:

Well, well; I no more will be a derider,
I did not look for such things from a spider.

Spider:

Come, hold thy peace; what I have yet to say,
If heeded, may help you another day.
Since I an ugly venomous creature be,
There is some semblance 'twixt vile man and me.

My wild and heedless runnings are like those
Whose ways to ruin do their souls expose.
Daylight is not my time, I work at night,

To show they are like me who hate the light.

The maid sweeps one web down, I make another,
To show how heedless ones convictions smother;
My web is no defence at all to me,
Nor will false hopes at judgment be to thee.

Sinner:

O spider, I have heard you, and do wonder
A spider should thus lighten and thus thunder!

Spider:

Do but hold still, and I will let you see
Yet in my ways more mysteries there be.
Shall not I do you good, if I you tell,
For, since I set my web in sundry places,
I show men go to hell in divers traces.

One I set **in the window**, that I might
Show some go down to hell with gospel light.

One I set **in a corner**, as you see,
To show how some in secret snared be.

Gross webs great store I set **in darksome places**,
To show how many sin with brazen faces;

Another web I set **aloft on high**,
To show there's some professing men must die.

Thus in my ways God wisdom does conceal,
And by my ways that wisdom does reveal.

I hide myself when I for flies do wait,
So does the devil when he lays his bait;
If I do fear the losing of my prey,
I stir me, and more snares upon her lay:
This way and that her wings and legs I tie,

That, sure as she is caught, so she must die.
But if I see she's like to get away,
Then with my venom I her journey stay.
All which my ways the devil imitates
To catch men, 'cause he their salvation hates.

Sinner:

O spider, you delight me with your skill!
I pray thee spit this venom at me still.

Spider:

I am a spider, yet I can possess
The palace of a king, where happiness
So much abounds.[1] Nor when I do go thither,
Do they ask what, or whence I come, or whither
I make my hasty travels; no, not they;
They let me pass, and I go on my way.

I seize the palace, do with hands take hold
Of doors, of lock, or bolts; yea, I am bold,
When in, to clamber up unto the throne,
And to possess it, as if 'twere mine own.

Nor is there any law forbidding me
Here to abide, or in this palace be.

Yea, if I please, I do the highest stories
Ascend, there sit, and so behold the glories
Myself is compassed with, as if I were
One of the chiefest courtiers that be there.

Here lords and ladies do come round about me,
With grave demeanour, nor do any flout me
For this, my brave adventure, no, not they;
They come, they go, but leave me there to stay.

---

1. "The spider skillfully grasps with its hands, and it is in the kings' palaces." Prov. 30:28

Now, my reproacher, I do by all this
Show how you may possess yourself of bliss:
You are worse than a spider, but take hold
On Christ the door, you shall not be controlled.

By Him do you the heavenly palace enter;
None will chide you for this your brave adventure;
Approach you then unto the very throne,
There speak your mind, fear not, the day's your own;
Nor saint, nor angel, will stop you or stay,
But rather tumble blocks out of the way.

My venom stops not me; let not your vice
Stop you; possess yourself of paradise.
Go on, I say, although you be a sinner,
Learn to be bold in faith, of me a spinner.

This is the way the glories to possess,
And to enjoy what no man can express.

Sometimes I find the palace door unlocked,
And so my entrance thither has unblocked.
But am I daunted? No, I here and there
Do feel and search; so if I anywhere,
At any chink or crevice, find my way,
I crowd, I press for passage, make no stay.

And so through difficulty I attain
The palace; yea, the throne where princes reign.
I crowd sometimes, as if I'd burst in sunder;
And are you crushed with striving, do not wonder.

Some scarce get in, and yet indeed they enter;
Knock, for they nothing have, that nothing venture.
Nor will the King himself throw dirt on thee,
As you have cast reproaches upon me.

He will not hate you, O you foul backslider!
As you did me, because I am a spider.

Now, to conclude: since I such doctrine bring,
Slight me no more, call me not ugly thing.
God's wisdom has unto the ant been given,
And spiders may teach men the way to heaven.

Sinner:

Well, my good spider, I my errors see,
I was a fool for railing upon thee.
Thy nature, venom, and thy fearful hue,
Both show what sinners are, and what they do.

Your way and works do also darkly tell,
How some men go to heaven, and some to hell.
You are my monitor, I am a fool;
I have now learned that to spiders go to school.

Questions on Poem VIII

Q. 1. Why does man despise the spider?
Q. 2. In what ways does the spider benefit the man?
Q. 3. How is the spider an object lesson of spiritual truth?

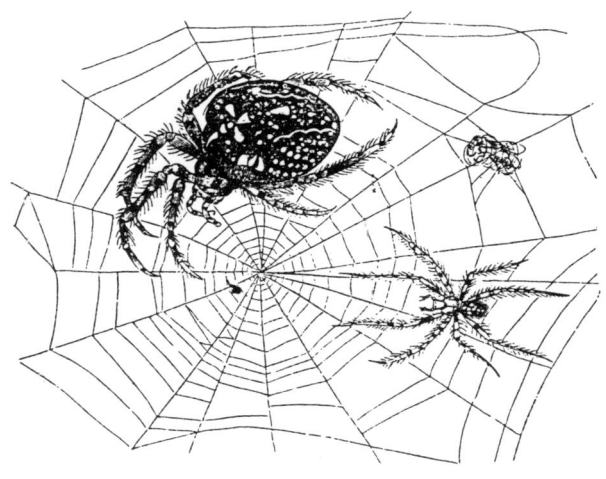

A Garden Spider

XIV

THE BEE

The bee goes out, and honey home does bring,
And some who seek that honey find a sting.
To get the honey, and to still be free
From stinging, you need first to kill the bee.

Comparison

This bee an emblem truly is of sin,
Whose honey, unto many, death hath been.
You cannot have sweet from sin and yet not die,
Unless your sin you first place, mortify.

Questions on Poem XIV

Q. 1. How does someone not dressed as a bee keeper get honey from a bee?

Q. 2. What spiritual lesson can be learned from the bee?

Lessons from Nature: Poems for Boys and Girls

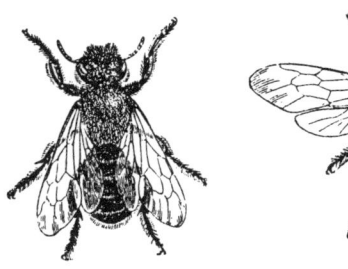

male bee   female bee

XV

THE ANT

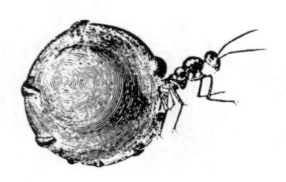

Must we from the tiny ant go to school[1],
To learn of her in summer to provide
For winter next ensuing? Man's a fool,
Or silly ants would not be made his guide.

But, sluggard, is it not a shame for thee
To be outdone by busy ants?[2] Pray hear:
Their works, too, will your condemnation be
When at the judgment-seat you shall appear.

But since your God does bid you to her go,
Obey, her ways consider, and be wise;
Ants plan and work hard together you know,
Setting a good example for our eyes.

---

1. Most ants can lift up to ten times their body weight and some can lift up to fifty times their body weight. --World Book

2. *Go to the ant, you sluggard! Consider her ways and be wise. Which, having no captain, overseer or ruler, provides her supplies in the summer, and gathers her food in the harvest.* --Proverbs 6:6-8

The ants are a people not strong, yet they prepare their food in the summer. --Proverbs 30:25

Lessons from Nature: Poems for Boys and Girls

Section of an ant hill

Questions Poem XV
Q. 1. What can we learn from the ant?
Q. 2. How do we tend to differ from the ant?

68

XVI

FISH IN THE WATER

The water is the fish's element;
Take her from thence, none can her death prevent;
Likewise, the proud transgressors soon must die
Who rule their life without the Lord on high.

The water is the fish's element;
Leave her but there, and she is well content.
So's he, who in the path of life does plod,
Take all, says he, let me but have my God.

The water is the fish's element,
Her sportings there to her are excellent
So is God's service unto holy men,
They are not in their element till then.

Questions on Poem XVI
Q. 1. Compare the fish and water to man and God?
Q. 2. How can we find the contentment of a fish in water?
Q. 3. Compare a fish in water to a believer in service to God?

catfish

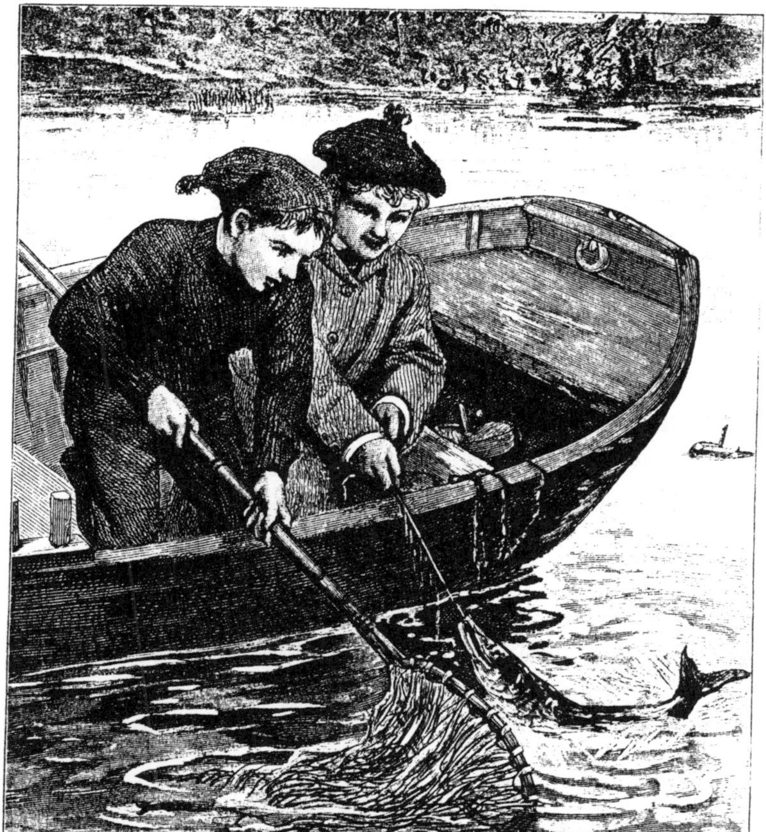

XVII

THE FLINT IN THE WATER

This flint, over time, has abode,
Where crystal streams make their continual road.
Yet it abides a flint as much as ever
Before it touched the water, or came there
Its constant hardness not abated,
'Tis not at all by water penetrated.
Though water hath a softening virtue in't,
This stone it can't dissolve, for 'tis a flint.

Yea, though it in the water does remain,
It does its fiery nature still retain.
If you oppose it with its opposite,
At you, yea, in your face, its fire 'twill spit.

Comparison

This flint an emblem is of those that lie
Like stones, under the Word, until they die.
Its crystal streams have not their nature changed,
They are not, from their lusts, by grace estranged.

Questions on Poem XVII

Q. 1. Describe the characteristics of a flint stone.
Q. 2. How is an unrepentant sinner like the flint?

Editor: Some people live and die without having their nature changed by the Scriptures. The imagery names two ways they compare to a flint in the water. They are hardened and untouched by the Word but in conflict with others.

XVIII

THE MOLE IN THE GROUND

The mole's a creature very smooth and slick,
She digs in dirt, but 'twill not on her stick;
So's he who counts this world his greatest gains,
Yet nothing gets but labour for his pains.

Earth's the mole's element, she can't abide
To be above ground, dirt heaps are her pride;
And he is like her who the worldling plays,
He imitates her in her work and ways.

Poor silly mole, that you should love to be
Where you no sun, nor moon, nor stars can see.

Comparison

How silly now the man who does not care
If he gets earth, to have of heaven a share!

Questions on Poem XVIII

Q. 1. Describe the mole?
Q. 2. What type of person is like a mole?

XIX

THE FROG

The frog by nature is both damp and cold,
Her mouth is large, her belly much will hold;
She sits somewhat ascending, loves to be
Croaking in gardens, though unpleasantly.

Comparison

The hypocrite is like unto this frog,
As like as is the puppy to the dog.

He is of nature cold, his mouth is wide
To chatter, and at goodness to deride.

He mounts his head as if he was above
The world, when yet 'tis that which has his love.

And though he seeks in churches for to croak,
He neither loves Jesus nor his yoke.

Questions on Poem XIX
Q. 1. Describe the characteristics of the frog.
Q. 2. How is a hypocrite like a frog?

Lessons from Nature: Poems for Boys and Girls

European edible frog

XX

THE DAY BEFORE SUNRISE

But all this while, where's he whose golden rays
Drives night away and beautifies our days?

Where's he whose goodly face doth warm and heal,
And show us what the darksome nights conceal?

Where's he that thaws our ice, drive cold away?
Let's have him, or we care not for the day.

Comparison

Thus 'tis with who partakers are of grace,
There's naught to them like their Redeemer's face.

Questions on Poem XX

Q. 1. Identify the characteristics of the sun in this poem.
Q. 2. A person desiring the rising of the sun is liken to whom? Compare with Psalm 130:5-6.

XXI

THE PEEP OF DAY

I oft, though it be peep of day, don't know
If night has come or the day will soon go.

I fancy that I see a little light,
But cannot distinguish day from night;

I hope, I doubt, but steady yet I be not,
I am not at a point, the sun I see not.

Thus 'tis with such who grace but now possessed [1]
They know not yet if they be cursed or blessed.

---

1. When divine light first dawns upon the soul to reveal sin, O how difficult is it to conclude that sin is pardoned, and the sinner blest! (Ed.)

Questions on Poem XXI

Q. 1. What two times of day are compared?

Q. 2. What spiritual application is made in this poem?

XXII

THE RISING OF THE SUN.

Look, look, brave Sun doth peep up from beneath,
Shows us his golden face, doth on us breathe;

He also doth compass us round with glories,
Whilst he ascends up to his highest stories.

Where he his banner over us displays,
And gives us light to see our works and ways.

Nor are we now, as at the peep of light,
To question, is it day, or is it night?

The night is gone, the shadows fled away,
And we now most sure are that it is day.

Our eyes behold it, and our hearts believe it;
Nor can the wit of man in this deceive it.

And thus it is when Jesus shows his face,
And does assure us of his love and grace.

Questions on Poem XXII
Q. 1. Contrast the rising of the sun with the peep of light?
Q. 2. What the characteristics of the risen sun?
Q. 3. What spiritual time is compared to sunrise? Explain.

XXIII

A LOWERING MORNING

Well, with the day I see the clouds appear,
And mix the light with darkness everywhere;
The weather threatens to travellers that go
Long journeys, pounding rain they'll have, or snow.

Else, while I gaze, the sun does with his beams
Belace the clouds, as 'twere with bloody streams;
This done, they suddenly do watery grow,
And weep, and pour their tears out where they go.

Comparison

Thus 'tis when gospel light does usher in
To us both sense of grace and sense of sin;

Yea, when it makes sin red with Christ's blood,
Then we can weep till weeping does us good.

Questions on Poem XXIII

Q. 1. When we give nature attributes of people, we call that personification. For example, "The trees shivered in the cold." How does Bunyan use personification in this poem?

Q. 2. How is weeping that leads to repentance (the weeping that does us good) profitable as opposed to weeping based only on frustration or disappointment?

XXIV

THE SUN'S REFLECTION UPON THE CLOUDS IN A FAIR MORNING

Look yonder, ah! methinks mine eyes do see
Clouds edged with silver, as fine garments be;
They look as if they saw that golden face
That makes black clouds most beautiful with grace.

Unto the saints' sweet incense, or their prayer,
These smoky curdled clouds I do compare.
For as these clouds seem edged, or laced with gold,
Their prayers return with blessings manifold.

Questions on Poem XXIV

Q. 1. How does Bunyan describe the sky in this poem?

Q. 2. To what are the clouds compared?

XXV

THE GOING DOWN OF THE SUN

What, hast thou turn thy race, art going down?
Thou seemest angry, why dost on us frown?
Yea, wrap thy head with clouds and hide thy face,
As threatening to withdraw from us thy grace?

O leave us not! When once thou hid'st thy head,
Our horizon with darkness with be spread.
Tell who hath thee then offended, turn again.
Alas! too late, entreaties are in vain.

Comparison

Our gospel has had here a summer's day,
But in its sunshine we, like fools, did play;
Or else fall out, and with each other wrangle,
And did, instead of work, not much but jangle.

And if our sun seems angry, hides his face,
Shall it go down, shall night possess this place?
Let not the voice of night birds us afflict,
And of our misspent summer us convict.

How agonizing will be the cry of the lost soul---' The harvest is past, the summer is ended, and we are not saved,' Jer. 8:20.--(Ed.)

Questions on Poem XXV

Q.1. How does Bunyan describe the setting of the sun?
Q. 2. What spiritual truth does the setting sun illustrate?

XXVI

A SNAIL

She goes slowly, but she does go for sure,
She stumbles not, as a stronger creature.
Her journey's shorter, so she may endure
Better than they whose distance outreach her.

She makes no noise, but stilly seizeth on
The flower or herb appointed for her food,
The which she quietly doth feed upon
While others range and glare, but find no good,
And though she doth but very softly go,
However, 'tis not fast nor slow, but sure;
And certainly they that do travel so,
The prize they do aim at they do procure.

Comparison

Although, they seem not much to stir, 'tis true,
To hunger for Christ or from His wrath flee,
Yet what they seek for quickly they come to,
Though it doth seem the farthest off to be.

One act of faith doth bring them to that flower
They so long for, that they may eat and live,
Which, to attain, is not in others power,
Though for it a king's ransom they would give.

Then let none faint, nor be at all dismayed
That life by Christ do seek, they shall not fail
To have it; let them nothing be afraid;
The herb and flower are eaten by the snail.

Lessons from Nature: Poems for Boys and Girls

A species of edible snail

    A snail is a slow crawling, small, soft-bodied mollusk. There are land snails, fresh water snails, and marine snails. Most snails have spiral coiled shells on their backs that they can draw into for protection.

If the crawling snail finds food, wherefore do you doubt, O! you of little faith?--(Ed.)

Questions on Poem XXVI
Q. 1. Describe the snail.
Q. 2. Who should the snail encourage? Why?
Q. 3. Can you make another analogy between the snail and the Christian life?

XXVII

A SKILLFUL PLAYER ON AN INSTRUMENT

He that can play well on an instrument,
Will take the ear, and captivate the mind
With mirth or sadness; for that it is bent
Thereto, as music in it place does find.

But if one hears that has therein no skill,
(As often music lights of such a chance)
Of its brave notes they soon be weary will:
And there are some can neither sing nor dance.

Comparison

Unto him that thus skilfully does play,
God does compare a gospel-minister,
That rightly preaches, and does godly pray,
Applying truly what does thence infer.

This man, whether of wrath or grace he preach,
So skillfully does handle every word;
Any by his saying does the heart so reach,
That it does joy or sigh before the Lord.

But some there be, which, as the brute, does lie
Under the Word, without the least advance
Godward; such do despise the ministry;
They weep not at it, neither to it dance.

Questions on Poem XXVII

Q. 1. What two types of people does Bunyan describe?
Q. 2. How does Bunyan compare the skillful player of music to the minister of the gospel?
Q. 3. How does he compare the listener of the music to the listener of the gospel?

XXVIII

A FIRE

Who falls into the fire shall burn with heat;
While those remote scorn from it to retreat.
Yea, while those in it, cry out, O! I burn,
Some farther off those cries to laughter turn.

Comparison

While some tormented are in hell for sin;
On earth some greatly do delight therein.
Yea, while some make it echo with their cry,
Other count it a fable and a lie.

Fools make a mock at sin. The scorner occupies a proud, an elevated seat, which will sink under him, and crush him down to everlasting destruction. The threatenings and promises of God stand sure for ever.--(Ed.)

Questions on Poem XXVIII

Q. 1. Bunyan lists two different reactions of people to fire. How does the person who has fallen in the fire differ from a person watching at a safe distance from a fire?

Q. 2. How does this apply to spiritual things?

XXIX

A CANDLE

Unlit Candles

    Man's like a candle in a candlestick,
    Made up of tallow and a little wick;
    And as the candle when it is not lighted,
    So is he who is in his sins benighted.

    Nor can a man his soul with grace inspire,
    More than can candles set themselves on fire.
    Candles receive their light from what they are not;
    Men grace from Him who at first they cared not.

The Master Caring for the Candle

    We manage candles when they take the fire;
    God manages the men his grace inspires.
    And biggest candles give the better light,
    As grace on biggest sinners shines most bright.

The Interworking of the Parts of a Candle

> Again, though it may seem to some a riddle,
> We use to light our candles at the middle. [1]
> True light doth at the candle's end appear,
> And grace the heart first reaches by the ear.
>
> But 'tis the wick the fire doth kindle on,
> As 'tis the heart that grace first works upon.
> Thus both do fasten upon what's the main,
> And so their life and vigor do maintain.

The tallow makes the wick yield to the fire,
And sinful flesh doth make the soul desire
That grace may kindle on it, in it burn;
So evil makes the soul from evil turn. [2]

The Function of a Candle

The candle shines to make another see,
A saint unto his neighbor light should be.
The blinking candle we do much despise,
Saints dim of light are high in no man's eyes.

Enemies of Candle Light

But candles in the wind are apt to flare,
And Christians, in a tempest, to despair.
The flame also with smoke attended is,
And in our holy lives there's much amiss.

Sometimes a thief will candle-light annoy,
And lusts do seek our graces to destroy.
What brackish is will make a candle sputter;
'Twixt sin and grace there's oft' a heavy clutter.

Sometimes the light burns dim, 'cause of the snuff,
Sometimes it is blown quite out with a puff;
But watchfulness prevents both these evils,
Keeps candles light, and grace in spite of devils.

Nor let not snuffs nor puffs make us to doubt,
Our candles may be lighted, though puffed out.
The candle in the night doth all excel,
Nor sun, nor moon, nor stars, then shine so well.

Comparison

So is the Christian in our hemisphere,
Whose light shows others how their course to steer.
When candles are put out, all's in confusion;
Where Christians are not, devils make intrusion.

Happy are all they who such candles place,
All others dwell in the darkness without grace.

But candles that do blink within the socket,
And saints, whose eyes are always in their pocket,
Are much alike; such candles make us fumble,
And at such saints good men and bad do stumble.[3]

Good candles don't offend, except sore eyes,
Nor hurt, unless it be the silly flies.
Thus none like burning candles in the night,
Nor ought [4] to holy living for delight.

Conclusion

But let us draw towards the candle's end:
The fire, you see, does wick and tallow spend,
As time man's life until his glass is run,
And so the candle and the man is done.

The man now lays him down upon his bed,
The wick yields up its fire, and so is dead.
The candle now extinct is, but the man
By grace mounts up to glory, there to stand.

1. This riddle is solved in the fourth line following. The light of the fear and love of God begins in the middle of our bodily frame, with the heart. Bunyan's love of religious riddles is seen in the second part of the Pilgrimage, when Christian is resting at the house of Gaius.--(Ed.)

2. Convictions of sin make the soul turn from sin.--(Ed.)

3. This character is admirably drawn in the second part of the *Pilgrim's Progress,* p. 200--Mr. Brisk, a suitor to Mercy.--(Ed.)

4. Preterite of the verb 'to save,' from the Saxon agan, to be held or bound by moral obligation.--Imperial Dictionary.--(Ed.)

XXX

THE FLY AT THE CANDLE

What ails this fly thus desperately to enter
A combat with the candle? Will she venture
To clash at light? Away, thou silly fly;
Thus doing thou will burn thy wings and die.

But 'tis a folly her advice to give,
She'll kill the candle, or she will not live.
Slap, says she, at it; then she makes retreat,
So wheels about, and doth her blows repeat.

Nor doth the candle let her quite escape,
But gives some little check unto the ape: [1]
Throws up her heels it doth, so down she falls,
Where she lies sprawling, and for relief calls.

When she recovers, up she gets again,
And at the candle comes with might and main,
But now behold, the candle takes the fly,
And holds her, till she doth by burning die.

Comparison

This candle is an emblem of that light
Our gospel gives in this our darksome night.
The fly a lively picture is of those
That hate and do this gospel light oppose.

At last the gospel doth become their snare,
Doth them with burning hands in pieces tear. [2]

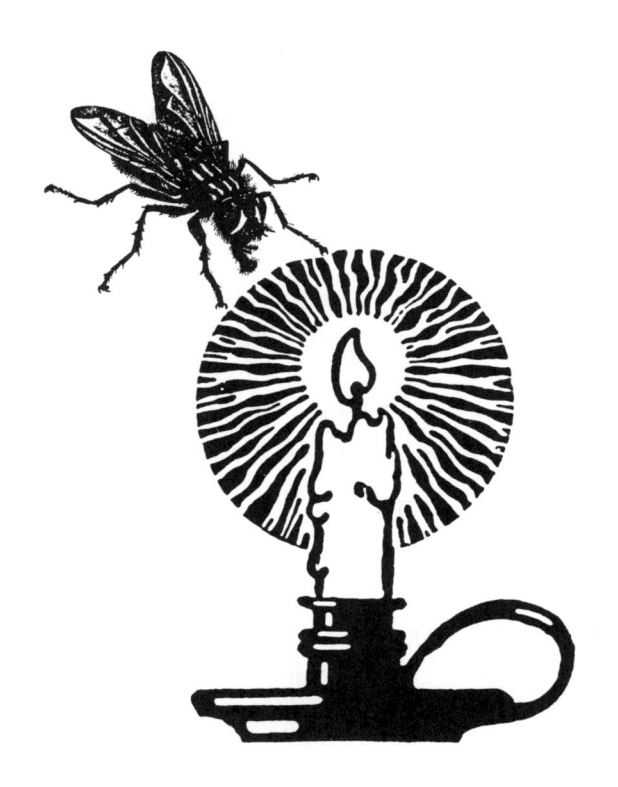

1. The word ape has four meanings, a certain kind of monkey, any monkey, a person who imitates, or the meaning used here in Bunyan's poem, a fool.
2. "To the one, a savour of death unto death; and to the other, a savour of life unto life," 2 Corinthians 2: 16.

Questions on Poem XXX
Q. 1. Have you ever watched a fly perform such a ritual with a candle as described here? Explain.
Q. 2. What spiritual truth does the candle represent? the fly?

XXXI

A POUND OF CANDLES FALLING TO THE GROUND

But be the candles down, and scattered too,
Some lying here, some there? What shall we do?

Hold, light the candle there that stands on high,
It you may find the other candles by.

Light that, I say, and so take up the pound
You did let fall and scatter on the ground.

Comparison

The fallen candles do us intimate
The bulk of God's elect in their laps'd state;
Their lying scattered in the dark may be
To show, by man's lapsed state, his misery.

The candle that was taken down and lighted,
Thereby to find them fallen and benighted,
Is Jesus Christ; God, by his light, does gather
Who he will save, to go unto the Father.

Questions on Poem XXXI

Q. 1. Describe the accident that inspired this poem.
Q. 2. What spiritual analogy does Bunyan make in this poem?

Lessons from Nature: Poems for Boys and Girls

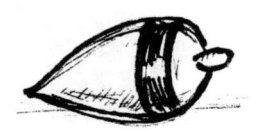

XXXII

THE SPINNING OF A TOP

'Tis with the string the boy sets up the top,
The whip makes it run round upon its toe;
The whip makes it hither and thither hop:
'Tis with the whip the top is made to go.

Comparison

Our legalist is like unto this top,
Without a whip he does not duty do;
Let Moses whip him, he will skip and hop;
Withdraw the whip, he'll neither stand nor go.

Questions on Poem XXXII

Q. 1. Self-control means to be internally controlled, not just subject to outside force. How does the top lack self-control?
Q. 2. In what way is a legalist like a top?

XXXIII

A PENNY LOAF

Thy price one penny is in time of plenty,
In famine doubled, 'tis from one to twenty.
Yea, no man knows what price on thee to set
When there is but one penny loaf to get.

Comparison

This loaf's an emblem of the Word of God,
A thing of low esteem before the rod
Of famine smites the soul with fear of death,
But then it is our all, our life, our breath.

When the Word of God dwells in us richly in all wisdom, then will the peace of God rule in our hearts, and we shall be sweet inclined to every good thought, word, and work.--(Ed.)

XXXIV

THE BEGGAR

He wants, he asks, he pleads his poverty,
They within doors do him an alms deny.
He does repeat and aggravate his grief,
But they repulse him, give him no relief.

He begs. They say, "Begone." He will not hear,
But coughs, sighs, and signals he is there;
They disregard him, he repeats his groans;
They still say nay, and he himself bemoans.

They grow more rugged, they call him vagrant;
He cries the shriller, trumpets out his want.
At last, when they perceive he'll take no nay,
An alms they give him without more delay.

Comparison

This beggar does resemble them that pray
To God for mercy, and will take no nay,
But wait, and count that all his hard gainsays
Are nothing else but fatherly delay;
Then imitate him, praying souls, and cry:
There's nothing like to importunity.

Questions on Poem XXXIV

Q. 1. What does importunity mean?
Q. 2. What because of the beggar's importunity?
Q. 3. How does Bunyan commends the same technique in partitioning a holy God?

Lessons from Nature: Poems for Boys and Girls

XXXV

THE THIEF

The thief, when he does steal, thinks he does gain;
Yet here the greatest loss he does sustain.
Come, thief, tell me your gain, but do not falter,
In summary what comes more than the halter?

Perhaps, you'll say, "Punishment I defy";
So you may say, yet by the noose will die.
You'll say, "Then there's an end"; no, pray you, hold,
He was no friend of yours that to you told.

Hear you the Word of God, that will you tell,
Without repentance thieves must go to hell.
But should it be as the false prophet says,
Yet naught but loss does come by thievish ways.

All honest men will flee your company,
You live a rogue, and so a rogue will die.
Innocent boldness you have none at all,
Your inward thoughts do you a villain call.

Sometimes when you lie warmly on your bed,
You are like one unto the gallows led.
Fear, as a constable, breaks in upon you,
When your sin is exposed what'll the town do?

If hogs do grunt, or silly rats do rustle,
You are in consternation, thinking a bustle
By men about the door, is made to take you,
And all because **good conscience does forsake you.**

Your case is most deplorably so bad,
You shun to think on it, lest you grow mad.
You are beset with mischiefs every way,
The gallows groan for you now every day.

Wherefore, I pray thee, thief, your theft forbear,
Consult your safety, learn to have a care.
If once your head be caught within the noose,
'Twill be too late a longer life to choose.

The Bible offers hope through penitence,
What's that to them who scoff at repentance?
Nor is God's grace at your command or power,
That you should put if off till the last hour.

I pray you, thief, repent, and turn betime;
Few live real long who do the gallows climb.

Questions on Poem XXXV

Q. 1. In what ways will a thief suffer?
Q. 2. What should the thief do to escape?

XXXVI

THE HORSE AND HIS RIDER

There's one rides very sagely on the road,
Showing that he affects the gravest mode.
Another rides tantivy [1], or full trot,
To show much gravity he matters not.

Lo, here come one amain[2], he rides full speed,
Hedge, ditch, nor miry bog, he does not heed.
One claws it up-hill without stop or check,
Another down as if he'd break his neck.
Every horse has his own special guider;
By his going you may know the rider.

Comparison

Now let us turn our horse into a man,
His rider to a spirit, if we can.
Let us, by methods of the guider,
Tell each horse how he can know his rider.

Some go, as men, direct in a right way,
Nor are they suffered to go astray;
As with a bridle they are governed,
And kept from paths which lead unto the dead.
Now this good man has his special guider,
Then by his going let him know his rider.

Some go as if they did not greatly care,
Whether of heaven or hell they should be heir.
The rein, it seems is laid upon their neck,
They seem to go their way without a check.
Now this man too has his special guider,
And by his going he may know his rider.

Some again run as if resolved to die,
Body and soul, to all eternity.

Good counsel they by no means can abide;
They'll have their course whatever them betide.
Now these poor men have their special guider,
Were they not fools they soon might know their rider.

There's one makes head against all godliness,
Those too, that profess it, he'll distress;
He'll taunt and flout if goodness does appear,
And at its countenancers [3] mock and jeer.
Now this man, too, has his special guider,
And by his going he might know his rider.

---

1. tantivy--a ride at full gallop, rush
2. amain--at full speed; in haste, at once; with full force
3. countenancers--persons who favor or encourage

XXXVII

A SHEET OF WHITE PAPER

This subject is unto the foulest pen,
Or fairest handled by the sons of men.
'Twill also show what is upon it writ.
Be it wisely, or nonsense for want of wit.

Each blot and blur it also will expose
To their next reader, be they friends or foes.

Comparison

Some souls are like unto this plain, blank sheet,
Though not in whiteness. The next man they meet,
If wise or fool, debauched or deluder,
Or what you will, the dangerous intruder
May write thereon, to cause that man to err
In doctrine or in life, with blot and blur.

Nor will that soul conceal from who observes,
But show how find it is, wherein it swerves

A reading man may know who was the writer,
And, by the hellish nonsense, the inditer.[1]

---

1. *inditer*-- one who puts words into writing or in a more obsolete sense, one who dictates or prescribes. Indite is the root word to inditement (the act of putting in words or writing).

XXXVIII

THE BOY AND WATCHMAKER

This watch my father did on me bestow,
A golden one it is, but 'twill not go,
Unless it be at an uncertainty:
But as good none as one to tell a lie.

When 'tis high day my hand will stand at nine;
I think there's no man's watch so bad as mine.
Sometimes 'tis sullen, 'twill not go at all,
Yet 'twas never broken nor had a fall.

Watchmaker

Your watch, though it be built with care and skill
May fail to do according to your will.

Suppose the balance, wheels, and springs be good,
And all things else, unless you understood
To manage it, as watches ought to be,
Your watch will still show you uncertainty.

Come, tell me, do you keep it from the dust?
And, do you wind it duly as you must?

Take heed, too, that you do not strain the spring;
You must be circumspect in everything;
Or else your watch, were it as good again,
Would not with time and tide you entertain.

Comparison

This boy an emblem is of a convert,
His watch of the work of grace within his heart.

The watch-maker is Jesus Christ our Lord,
His counsel, the directions of his Word.

Then convert, if thy heart be out of frame,
Of this watch-maker learn to mend the same.

Do not lay open thy heart to worldly dust,
Nor let thy graces over-grow with rust,
Be oft' renewed in spirit of thy mind,
Or else uncertain thou thy watch will find.

Watches once had to be hand wound. The owner could be careless and wind the watch too tightly and break the watch springs. (Ed.)

Questions on Poem XXXVIII

Q. 1. It is always the fault of the watchmaker if the timepiece does not do its job properly?
Q. 2. Describe the spiritual analogy based on the boy and the watchmaker.

XXXIX

AN HOUR-GLASS

This glass, when made, was, by the workman's skill,
The sum of sixty minutes to fulfill.
Time, more nor less, by it will out be spun,
But just an hour, and then the glass is run.

Comparison

Man's life we will compare unto this glass,
The number of his months he cannot pass;
But when he has accomplished his day,
He, like a vapor, vanishes away.

Questions on Poem XXXIX

Q. 1. The modern reader is not as acquainted with the hour-glass as the readers in John Bunyan's day. How is this like smaller replicas used to time turns in games, or with egg timers which measure the time it takes to boil an egg?
Q. 2. Read the following verses and explain what they mean in light of this poem: Psalm 90: 10, 12-14; 102:11; and James 4:14.

Lessons from Nature: Poems for Boys and Girls

XL

OVER-MUCH NICENESS

'Tis much to see how over nice some are
About their body home or car,[1]
While what's of worth they neglect mightily,
Not doing, or doing it carelessly.

Their house well furnished, with the latest print,
Meanwhile their soul lies bear, has no good in't.
Its outside also they must beautify,
When in it there's small effort made, a sigh.

Their bodies they must have tricked up and trim,
Their inside full of filth up to the brim.
Upon their clothes there must not be a spot,
But is their lives more than one common blot?

How nice, how coy are some about their diet,
But can their crying souls with hogs' meat quiet?
All groomed must their hair be, else 'tis naught
While of the living bread they have no thought.

**Thus for their outside they are clean and nice,
While their poor inside stinks with sin and vice.**

---

1. We made an editorial change from "about the body and household affair" to "about their body, home, or car." They did not have cars in Bunyan's life but the rhyme is better and the meaning more clear and relevant today.

Questions on Poem XL

Q. 1. Is Bunyan criticizing those who try to be clean and nice? Why or why not?
Q. 2. What is his main concern?
Q. 3. How is the theme of this poem similar to the accusation Jesus makes in Matthew 23:27-33?

XLI

APPAREL

God gave us clothes to hide our nakedness,
And we by them do it expose to view.
Our pride and unclean minds to an excess,
By our apparel, we to others show.

This is one of Bunyan's keen, shrewd, home thrusts. Clothes professedly made to hide what they studiously display!!--(Ed.)

Questions on Poem XLI
Q. 1. How can we use clothes to expose our sinful hearts?
Q. 2. Define immodesty. What is indecent attire? What type of dress would be defrauding to men outside of marriage?

XLII

A LOOKING-GLASS

In this see your beauty, have you any,
Or your defects, be they few or many.
You may, too, here your spots and freckles see,
Use your eyes, and count what their numbers be.
But are you blind? There is no looking-glass
Can show you your defects, your spots, or face.

Comparison

Unto this glass we may compare the Word,
For that to man's advantage does afford
(Has he a mind to know himself and state),
To see what will be his eternal fate.

But without eyes, alas! how can he see?
Many that seem to look ere, blind men be.
This is the reason they so often read
Their judgment there, and do it nothing dread.

Questions on Poem XLII
Q. 1. Why is a mirror a useless object for a blind man?
Q. 2. To what does Bunyan liken the mirror? Explain.

XLIII

MAN BY NATURE.

From God he's a backslider,
Of ways he loves the wider;
With wickedness a sider,
More venom than a spider.

In sin he's a considerer,
A make-bate[1] and divider;
Blind reason is his guider,
The devil is his rider.

black widow spider

---

1. make-bate-- an archaic expression meaning a person or thing that causes great trouble, leads to fighting, etc. Example: *It was ten to one if god, which was the make-bate of the world, did not... set us together by the ears.*--Daniel Defoe. [< make + (de)bate (strive)]

Question on Poem XLIII
Q. What characteristics are listed regarding man's nature?

XLIV

THE DISOBEDIENT CHILD

Children become, while little, our delight!
When they grow bigger, they begin to fright.
Their sinful nature prompts them to rebel,
And to delight in paths that lead to hell.

Their parents' love and care they overlook,
As if relation had them quite forsook.
They take the counsels of the wanton, rather
Than the most grave instructions of a father.

They reckon parents ought to do for them,
Though they the fifth commandment do condemn;
They snap and snarl if parents them control,
Though but in things most hurtful to the soul.

They reckon they are master, and that we
Who parents are, should to them subject be!
If parents fain would have a hand in choosing,
The children have a heart will in refusing.

They'll by wrong doing, under parents gather,
And say it is no sin to rob a father.
They'll jostle parents out of place and power,
They'll make themselves the head, and them devour.

How many children, by becoming head,
Have brought their parents to a piece of bread!
Thus they who, at the first, were parents' joy,
Turn that to bitterness, themselves destroy.

But, wretched child, how can you thus requite
Thy aged parents, for that great delight
They took in you, when you, as helpless, lay
In their indulgent bosoms day by day?

Your mother, long before she brought you forth,
Took care you should want neither food nor cloth.
Your father glad was at his very heart,
Had he to you a portion to impart.

Comfort they promised themselves in thee,
But you, it seems, to them a grief will be.
How oft how willingly brake they their sleep,
If you, their bantling, did but winch or weep.

Their love to you was such they could have given,
That you might live, almost their part of heaven.

But now, behold how they rewarded are!
For their indulgent love and tender care;
All is forgot, this love he does despise.
They brought this bird up to pick out their eyes.

Questions on Poem XLIV

Q. 1. In what ways can children turn from a delight to a fright?

Q. 2. What responsibility and subsequent blessing comes from obedience and honor given to parents (Exodus 20: 12; Ephesians 6:1-3).

XLV

THE LOVE OF CHRIST

The love of Christ, poor I may touch upon;
But 'tis unsearchable! O, there is none
Its large dimensions can comprehend
Should they dilate thereon world without end.

When we had sinned, in His zeal He sware,
That He upon His back our sins would bear.
And since unto sin is entailed death,
He vowed for our sins He'd lose his breath.

He did not only promise or resolve,
But to astonishment did so involve
Himself in man's distress and misery,
As for, and with him, both to live and die.

To His eternal fame in sacred story,
We find that He did lay aside his glory,
Stepped from the throne of highest dignity,
Became poor man, did in a manger lie;
Was beholden to others for His bread,
Had, of His own, no where to lay His head;
Though rich, He did for us become thus poor,
That he might make us rich for evermore.
Nor was this but the least of what He did,
But the outside of what he suffered.

God made His blessed Son under the law,
Under the curse, which, like the lion's paw,
Did rent and tear His soul for mankind's sin,
More than if we for it in hell had been.
His cries, His tears, and bloody agony,
The nature of His death does testify.
Nor did He of constraint Himself thus give,
For sin, to death, that man might with Him live.

He did do what He did most willingly,
He sung, and gave God thanks, that He must die.

Do kings usually die for captive slaves?
Yet we were such when Jesus died to save.
Yea, when He made Himself a sacrifice,
His enemies He sought to save weren't nice.

And though He was provoked to retract
His blest resolves for such so good an act,
By the abusive carriages of those
That did both Him, His love, and grace oppose;

Yet He, as unconcerned with such things,
Goes on, **determines to make captives kings**;
Yea, many of His murderers He takes
Into His favor, and them princes makes.

I will have mercy on her who had not obtained mercy; then I will say to those who were not My people, 'You are My people!" and they shall say, 'You are my God!
                                                            --Hosea 2:23

For as many as are led by the Spirit of God, these are sons of God. For you did not receive the spirit of bondage again to fear, but you received the Spirit of adoption by whom we cry out, 'Abba, Father.'
                                                            --Romans 8:14-15

XLVI

MOSES AND HIS WIFE

This Moses, the lawgiver, was a pale man,
His wife a dark-skinned Ethiopian;
Their marriage did not change his milk-white skin;
She came out thence as black as she went in.

Comparison

God's law is very holy, just, and good,
And to it is espoused[1] all flesh and blood;
But this its goodness the law can't bestow
On any wedded to it here below.

Therefore as Moses' wife came swarthy[2] in,
And went out from him without change of skin,
So he that does the law for life adore,
His nature by it won't change evermore.

---

1. espoused--married to, bound to
2. swarthy--having dark skin

Note: We should not confuse the symbolism here as making any value distinction between different racial colors. Our true value comes from our spiritual state, not our skin tone.

Questions on Poem XLVI

Q. 1. What did not change by the marriage of Moses and his wife?
Q. 2. How does Bunyan describe the law?
Q. 3. What is the Law designed to do? See Romans 3:20 and Romans 8:3-4.

XLVII

THE SPOUSE OF CHRIST

Who's this that cometh from the wilderness,
Like smoky pillars thus perfumed with myrrh,
Leaning upon her dearest in distress,
Led into's bosom by the Comforter?

She's clothed with the sun, crowned with twelve stars,
The spotted moon her footstool she had made.
The dragon her assaults, fills her with jars,
Yet she rests she under her Beloved's shade.

But whence was she? what is her pedigree?
Was not her father a poor Amorite?
What was her mother but as others be,
A poor, a wretched, and a sinful Hittite.

Yea, as for her, the day that she was born,
As loathsome, out of doors they did her cast;
Naked and filthy, stinking and forlorn;
This was her pedigree from first to last.

Nor was she pitied in the estate,
All let her lie polluted in her blood:
None her condition did commiserate,
There was no heart that sought to do her good.

Yet she unto these ornaments is come,
Her breasts are fashioned, her hair is grown;
She is made heiress of the best kingdom;
All her indignities away are blown.

Cast out she was, but now she home is taken,
Naked (sometimes), but now, you see, she's clothed;
Now made the darling, though before forsaken,
Barefoot, but now as princes' daughters shod.

Husbands love your wives, just as Christ also loved the church and gave Himself for it, that He might sanctify and cleanse it with the washing of water by the word, that He might present it to Himself a glorious church, not having spot or wrinkle or any such thing, but that it should be holy and without blemish.
                                                            --Ephesians 5:25-27

Instead of filth, she now has her perfumes;
Instead of ignominy, her chains of gold:
Instead of what the beauty most consumes,
Her beauty's perfect, lovely to behold.

Those that attend and wait upon her be
Princes of honor, clothed in white array;
Upon her head's a crown of gold, and she
Eats wheat, honey, and oil, from day to day.

For her beloved, he's the highest of all,
The only Potentate, the King of kings:
Angels and men do him Jehovah call,
And from him life and glory always springs.

He's white and ruddy, and of all the chief:
His head, his locks, his eyes, his hands, and feet,
Do, for completeness, out-go all belief;
His cheeks like flowers are, his mouth most sweet.

As for his wealth, he is made heir of all;
What is in heaven, what is on earth is his:
And be this lady his joint-heir does call,
Of all that shall be, or at present is.

Well, lady, well, God has been good to thee;
You of an outcast, now are made a queen.
Few, or none, may with thee compared be,
A beggar made thus high is seldom seen.

Take heed of pride, remember what thou art
By nature, though you have in grace a share,
You in yourself do yet retain a part
Of your own filthiness; wherefore beware.

Questions on Poem XLVII

Q. 1. Who is the spouse of Christ?
Q. 2. Why does Bunyan warn this bride to avoid pride?

XLVIII

THE SACRAMENTS

Two sacraments I do believe there be,
Baptism and the Supper of the Lord;
Both mysteries divine, which do to me,
By God's appointment, benefit afford.

But shall they be my God, or shall I have
Of them so foul and impious[1] a thought,
To think that from the curse they can me save?
Bread, wine, nor water, me no ransom bought.

---

1. impious--not pious; not having or showing reverence for God; wicked or profane

2. What folly, nay madness, for man to pretend to make God of a little flour, or to rely for forgiveness of sin on a wafer, a bit of bread, or a little wine or water. How degraded is he that pretends to believe such palpable absurdities.--(Ed.)

XLIX

THE LORD'S PRAYER IN RHYME

Our Father which in heaven art,
Thy name be always hallowed;
Thy kingdom come, thy will be done;
Thy heavenly path be followed.
By us on earth as 'tis with thee,
We humbly pray;
And let our bread us given be,
From day to day.
Forgive our debts as we forgive
Those that to us indebted are:
Into temptation lead us not,
But save us from the wicked snare.
The kingdom's thine, the power too.
We thee adore;
The glory also shall be thine
For evermore.

Amen.

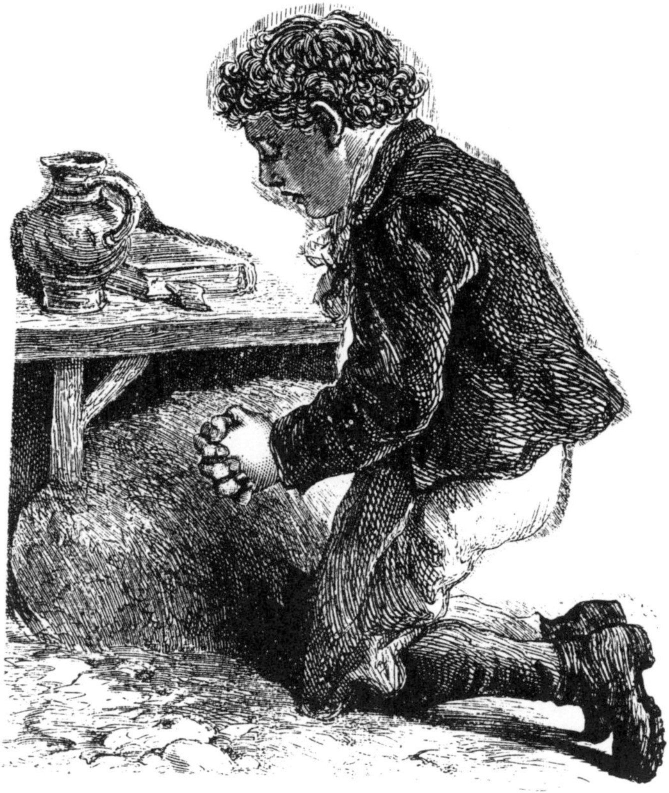